A BLAST WITH GLASS

PATHFINDER EDITION

By Macon Morehouse and Patrick McGeehan

CONTENTS

Cooking with Glass

By Macon Morehouse and Patrick McGeehan

Strong but breakable?
See-through yet solid like a wall?
Discover the secrets—and science—behind one of the
most beautiful and useful substances on Earth: glass.

A blast of heat greets you as you enter the hot shop. You feel as though you are standing on the edge of a volcano. Inside a furnace, or oven, molten goo glows like lava. It oozes like honey.

Perfect. Now you're cooking! But this is no ordinary recipe. When that goo cools and hardens, you'll see one of the most beautiful and useful materials on Earth: glass.

This hot shop belongs to Dale Chihuly, an artist famous for gorgeous glass sculptures. Here, glassblowers carefully shape hot glass into globes, curlicues, and swirls. Chihuly uses the pieces to make fanciful, rainbow-colored confections or creations. You can see one from a glass-topped bridge in Tacoma, Washington. Look up. The ceiling of the bridge looks like a sea of glass jellyfish.

Counting on Glass

Now take a look around you. Count all the things you see that are made of glass. Are you gazing out a window? Sipping water from a "glass"? Turning on a light bulb?

Check out your television, computer, cell phone—even your skateboard. Yes, they all have glass parts. Glass is so useful, it's hard to imagine everyday life without it.

Glass also can connect us to worlds large and small. Glass lenses in telescopes let us peer far into space. Glass fibers carry thousands of phone, TV, and Internet signals into our homes. Each fiber is as thin as a hair! Then there are things too tiny for our eyes to see—that is until you look through a microscope lens made of, you guessed it, glass.

Gorgeous Glass. *Artist Dale Chihuly makes glass flow into amazing shapes.*

Glass Network. *Thin glass fibers carry data for phones, TVs, and computers.*

The Science of Glass

How can glass do so many things? It's because it's one of the most **versatile** materials in the world. Glass can be fragile, or easy to break—watch out for shattered, or broken, glass! Yet glass also can be strong enough to protect you from wind and rain. It even can be stronger than steel. Cooled glass feels hard. Still, heat it up, and it can ooze into different shapes.

What drew Chihuly to glass? "It is the most mysterious and magical of all materials," he says. He remembers the awe he felt seeing light pour through a stained-glass window. "When you're looking at glass," he says, "you're really looking at light."

It takes creativity to figure out all the things you can do with glass. To really cook with glass, you need science. Start with **physics** and this question: How does glass let light shine through? The secret lies in its **state of matter**.

Clear Colors. *Light from stained-glass windows makes colorful patterns.*

A Pinch of Physics

In some ways, glass is like a solid because it feels rigid and hard like a rock, and its shape doesn't change. Yet glass can act like a liquid. Remember that blob of hot goo? It flows smoothly and changes shape.

Here's the weird part: Even when glass cools and hardens, it's still like a liquid. It isn't runny like, say, water. The similarity lies inside glass, in tiny invisible particles called **atoms**.

In solids, atoms pack tightly together in neat, regular patterns. They are like well-behaved sports fans, seated in perfect rows at a game. Now imagine it's the end of the game and all the fans spill out into the parking lot. They are in a contained area, but they're scattered, or spread apart. That's like the atoms in a liquid.

Running Hot and Cold

As glass melts, its atoms get just as active and scattered as the moving sports fans. As glass cools, though, the atoms race to get into a solid's regular pattern, but they don't make it! The glass hardens too fast, and the atoms get stuck in place. They're still scattered, not tightly packed. So space remains between the scattered atoms—enough to let light through.

Because hardened glass is like a solid *and* a liquid, scientists have special names for it. Some call it a supercooled liquid. Others call it an amorphous solid—a solid without a set shape of its own. Chihuly just calls it cool.

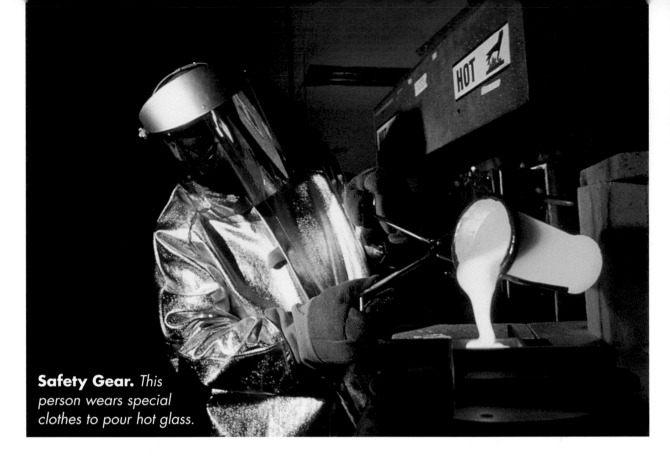

Safety Gear. *This person wears special clothes to pour hot glass.*

A Sprinkle of Chemistry

Physics helps explain glass. So does **chemistry**. Like a chef, a glass artist has to mix together and cook just the right ingredients to whip up a perfect batch of glass.

First comes silica, a very pure type of sand. Chihuly says it still amazes him to think that glass is made from "the most common material in the world." But wait! It's not so easy. It takes a fire at nearly 2,000°C (3,600°F) to melt silica. That's way too hot to handle!

Next, add a powder called soda. It's made from a kind of salt or the ashes of plants. The soda helps the silica melt at 1,200°C (2,200°F). Even at that lower temperature, the furnace is still four times as hot as a pizza oven. The soda, however, creates a new problem. It makes glass weak and allows it to dissolve, or get soft, in water. Imagine trying to drink out of that glass!

It takes a third ingredient to make glass strong and water resistant: a chalky powder called lime. Glass made with soda and lime is the most common kind of glass. It's used for windows, light bulbs, jars, and Chihuly's art.

Season with Color

Now you can add in a few extra ingredients. Want color? Try throwing in some different kinds of metals. Gold makes glass reddish, while iron gives glass a pale green color. For a middle-of-the-ocean kind of blue, glass artists use a substance called cobalt.

Maybe you want clear glass with sparkle and glitz, instead. Believe it or not, adding lead to your glass mixture does the trick. That recipe makes a fine crystal that shines like a flawless, shimmering diamond.

To make glass extra strong, you can add yet another substance called boron. Boron glass won't crack when you quickly change its temperature by moving it from a cool countertop to a hot oven or vice versa. That makes boron glass a perfect container for baking brownies. Now that's a great recipe!

And Bake

After mixing all the ingredients together, it's time to bake the glass mixture. High heat turns all the solid ingredients into a molten liquid. It can take as long as 24 hours for the ingredients to melt into a thick goo. Finally, it's time to turn this goo into art.

Step back into Chihuly's hot shop. Watch as a glassblower dips a hollow, metal pipe into the furnace and gathers a gob of molten glass. He blows and twirls, blows and twirls. The glass on the end of the pipe balloons out like a bubblegum bubble. As it cools, it becomes more viscous, or thicker. It flows more slowly. Now the glass is more like sticky, stretchy taffy.

The glass is getting harder to shape. But the piece isn't finished yet. The glassblower slips it into the glory hole, a small opening in the furnace. The intense heat softens the glass again. Now it's elastic, or stretchy, enough to keep blowing and shaping. What hard work!

The Cool Down

The piece is almost finished. It's just the right shape. For the final step, the glass art goes into an oven set to about 480°C (900°F). The oven and the glass will slowly cool down to room temperature. The glass will become stiff and hard. Don't skip this step. If hot glass cools too quickly, disaster strikes. It explodes!

Even the best glassblowers face this problem. "Don't even talk to me!" Chihuly says. He's joking—sort of. It turns out he'd recently worked with a great glassblower from Italy. They made two beautiful glass sculptures. "We cooled them too fast and they broke!" Chihuly says.

It typically takes overnight to cool a Chihuly piece. The bigger the piece, the longer it takes. In the 1930s, the Corning Glass Company made a glass mirror for a giant telescope in California. The mirror was 5 meters (17 feet) wide and took ten months to cool!

Floating Art. *Glass balls, flowers, and twisty stalks turn a boat into a sea of color.*

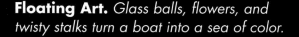

A Window on Glass

Ever since people first created glass 5,000 years ago, they've pushed its limits. Could it be used to make bigger, stronger, more delicate, or more useful things? Yes, glass could do all that—and more! Over time, glass changed the way we live.

Up until the first century B.C.E., glass pieces were made slowly and painstakingly. It could take days to make a single glass bottle. Then the Romans developed a way to blow glass, and suddenly glass became part of everyday life. Glassblowers crafted drinking cups, food containers, and jars to hold perfume. Glass urns even held the ashes of the dead. You didn't have to be wealthy to afford these glass items.

The Romans also figured out how to make windows. For the first time, people could be inside and protected from bad weather—and see outside. The idea spread. At first, only the rich could afford windows. For centuries, you had to visit the villa of a wealthy family, a castle, or a church to find a window to peer through.

Today, windows and other glass items like light bulbs are mass-produced, or made in large numbers, in factories. That makes them less expensive. Many people can afford to buy them. We can light the dark corners of our homes. We can read in bed, even—*shhhh!*—under the covers. Our houses, schools, and cars all have glass windows. Some skyscrapers are wrapped almost completely in glass. What a view, inside and out!

Shattering Limits

Scientists and artists keep pushing the limits of glass. How? Take a trip to the Indianapolis Children's Museum. You'll find a twisting, candy-colored tower that rises 13 meters (43 feet) into the air. It weighs 8,165 kilograms (9 tons). Above the tower floats a ceiling filled with swirling shapes. It took 5,000 pieces of glass to create Chihuly's "Fireworks of Glass," one of the world's largest glass sculptures.

Can you imagine walking on a glass sidewalk staring into a chasm below? Visit the Grand Canyon's Skywalk. Look down past your feet to the river 1.2 kilometers (nearly a mile) below. Only a shelf of clear glass, eight centimeters (three inches) thick, holds you up. Or go to a zoo where just a sheet of glass separates you from the tigers. Who's looking at whom?

Glass keeps astronauts safe, too. A special glass coating protects the space shuttle from burning as it speeds through the sky. Now that's an out-of-this-world use of glass!

What will scientists come up with next? Imagine diving deep into the ocean in a glass submarine. Wouldn't the undersea views be amazing? Or fly in an airplane with glass wings! Clothes made from glass fibers could make you almost invisible. Are these ideas far-fetched? They're not. Glass may be an ancient material, but it's clear: We're still cooking with glass!

Everyday Glass. *Ancient Romans made these glass containers.*

Globe of Glass. *At Boston's Mapparium, a three-story glass globe lets you see the world in a whole new way.*

Sky High Glass. *This towering skyscraper looks wrapped in glass. Imagine the view from the top floor!*

Wordwise

atom: smallest part of a substance that has all the traits of that substance

chemistry: study of the structure of substances and how they change

physics: study of forces and how they change an object's shape and motion

state of matter: physical property that describes a substance such as solid, liquid, or gas

versatile: can be used in many different ways

NATURE'S GLASS

Look at the world around you. Glass is everywhere! Glass made by people gets used everyday. But did you know that nature makes glass, too? High heat from meteors, lightning, and volcanoes can turn sand into glass.

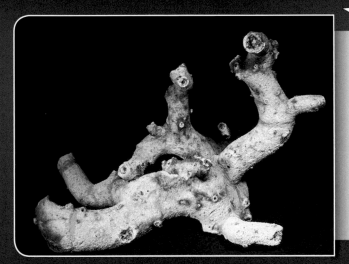

Lightning strikes. When it hits a desert or a beach, the heat can melt the sand and create something called a fulgurite. It's also called petrified lightning. Fulgurites resemble hollow tree branches. They're sandy on the outside, but look inside and you'll see shiny glass. But be careful because fulgurites can be fragile. One touch, and they may crumble.

BAM!

A meteorite, or chunk of burning space rock, slams into Earth. Scientists think that the heat produced during these collisions can make glass. They've found button-shaped glass discs called tektites in at least four places on Earth. The oldest known tektites, which are 35 million years old, were discovered in Texas.

POW!

A volcano erupts and hot, liquid rock flows. Then it quickly cools. What happens if some of that rock has a lot of silica, or sand, in it? It can turn to glass. This kind of glass is called obsidian, and it's often shiny and black. Native Americans used obsidian to make tools and weapons such as arrowheads.

Glittering Glass

Start cooking with glass to answer these questions.

1 Why is glass important for everyday life?

2 How is glass like both a solid and a liquid?

3 How is glass made? List the steps in order.

4 Today, glass items are mass-produced. Define *mass-produced.*

5 Descibe three kinds of glass made by nature.